MEDIA, FEMINISM, CULTURAL STUDIES

Stepping Forward: Essays, Lectures and Interviews
by Wolfgang Iser

Wild Zones: Pornography, Art and Feminism
by Kelly Ives

Global Media Warning: Explorations of Radio, Television and the Press
by Oliver Whitehorne

Andrea Dworkin
by Jeremy Mark Robinson

Cixous, Irigaray, Kristeva: The Jouissance of French Feminism
by Kelly Ives

Sex in Art: Pornography and Pleasure in Painting and Sculpture
by Cassidy Hughes

*The Erotic Object: Sexuality in Sculpture
From Prehistory to the Present Day*
by Susan Quinnell

Women in Pop Music
by Helen Challis

Detonation Britain: Nuclear War in the UK
by Jeremy Mark Robinson

Julia Kristeva: Art, Love, Melancholy, Philosophy, Semiotics
by Kelly Ives

Luce Irigaray: Lips, Kissing, and the Politics of Sexual Difference
by Kelly Ives

Helene Cixous I Love You: The Jouissance of Writing
by Kelly Ives

The Poetry of Cinema
by John Madden

The Sacred Cinema of Andrei Tarkovsky
by Jeremy Mark Robinson

Disney Business, Disney Films, Disney Lands
Daniel Cerruti

Feminism and Shakespeare
by B.D. Barnacle

Discovering the Goddess

Discovering the Goddess

A Personal Testimony

GEOFFREY ASHE

CRESCENT MOON

CRESCENT MOON PUBLISHING
P.O. Box 393
Maidstone
Kent, ME14 5XU
United Kingdom

First published 1995. Second edition 2007.
© Geoffrey Ashe 1995, 2007.

Printed and bound in Great Britain.
Set in Garamond Book 10 on 14pt.
Designed by Radiance Graphics.

The right of Geoffrey Ashe to be identified as the author of *Discovering the Goddess* has been asserted generally in accordance with sections 77 and 78 of the Copyright, Designs and Patents Act 1988.

All rights reserved. No part of this book may be reprinted or reproduced, stored in a retrieval system, or transmitted, in any form or by any means, electronic, mechanical, photocopying, recording or otherwise, without permission from the publisher.

British Library Cataloguing in Publication data available for this title

Ashe, Geoffrey
Discovering the Goddess: Personal Testimony
I. Title
291.2114

ISBN 1-86171-195-6
ISBN-13 9781-861711953

Contents

Discovering the Goddess   11

Bibliography   29

Illustrations   33

Leonardo da Vinci, *The Virgin of the Rocks*, National Gallery, London

In the summer of 1993 a 'Parliament of Religions' met in Chicago to mark the centenary of a similar gathering. Two speakers expounded a topic that was not on the agenda the first time: the religion of the goddess. The Pope had just been deploring its inroads among American Catholic women. Over the past fifteen years or so, resurgent Goddess-worship has grown into a live issue, chiefly in the United States. But not solely in the United States. And some of its antecedents are in Britain, and farther back. Mention might be made of the esoteric novelist Dion Fortune; also, surprisingly, Bernard Shaw. I have my own interest here. Whether there is occult significance in the fact that I live in Dion Fortune's house, I cannot say. I certainly never lived in Shaw's.

At Portland State University, Oregon, I give a summer course as a visiting professor, on Goddess myth and history and the implications. When I launched it in 1990 it was, to the best of my knowledge, the only course of its kind at any such institution. Possibly it still is. Looking back over the involvement that has led me to it, I realize that this has been very long and rather curious, and that it sheds light on one or two little-publicized factors in the Goddess movement. Since the movement seems to have to stay, I think the story worth telling. I have never told it in print before.

It begins in the 1940s when I was an incipient writer, hardly beyond the stage of doing the odd book-review. My first original piece with any substance was an article on Robert Graves's historical novels, which enthralled me, especially *I, Claudius* and *Claudius the God*. My article was published in *Tribune*, then a serious weekly of which Orwell had lately been literary editor. The BBC made use of it. I sent a copy to Graves in Majorca. He replied with an extraordinary letter, running back and forth and up and down on one flimsy sheet of paper. The article, he said, was the first study of his novels that anybody had written. Among several abrupt questions and unconnected remarks, he mentioned an impending new book of his, based, he told me, on a complicated Welsh riddle. I could make nothing of his account of this. When it appeared, it turned out to be *The White Goddess*. It was ahead of its time. As is well known, Graves's usual publishers turned it down. But the book came into its own in the Goddess revival, which it helped to inspire.

Like many readers, I had great difficulty with it. Eventually I more or less grasped what Graves was driving at, including the idea – later developed by him and others, and now widely current – that all the Goddess-figures of myth and cult are aspect or manifestations of 'the Goddess', the ultimate female Power or Energy, hinted at in Goethe's *Ewig-Weibliche* at the end of *Faust*: once accorded supreme honour under countless names and in countless forms, but pushed into the background by male deities, demoted and split up...to humanity's loss. The Goddess is not thought of as simply God with a gender change, she is different in kind. She is within Nature, not 'external to it' she is the Earth-Mother, with priority over the Sky-Father, who is an usurper; she is the universal life-giver, mistress of animals, Muse of inspiration, creator and destroyer; to be encountered, not argued about metaphysically. Pascal wrote that the God of his mystical experience was not the God of the philosophers. Anyone claiming acquaintance with the goddess would find such a distinction meaningless. There has never been a Goddess of the philosophers. It is doubtful whether there could be, in Pascal's sense.

To revert to my story, before I had got far with the Goddess (at that time, very few people had), a more familiar theme began to converge. During 1956 I lived for some months, with my wife and children, in the restored Carmelite community at Aylesford in Kent. Aylesford is the one place in England where a religious order recovered the house which it lost at the Reformation. The community was still overshadowed by the charisma of its founder, Father Malachy Lynch. He was deeply and cheerfully devoted to the Virgin Mary; a Protestant might have called him a Mariolater, and so, indeed, might some Catholics. He spoke of Our Lady more often than he spoke of Our Lord, extolling her celestial glories and loving-kindness and power, and never, so far as I recall, treating her in her earthly setting as a mere model of chastity or humility. In his eyes she was intensely real and, through her devotees, intensely active; he urged people to salute her each morning with the words 'Use me today'. The Second Vatican Council had not yet applied the brakes to Marian extremism, which, as Pope John XXIII remarked, has historically been apt in practice to put the Mother above the Son.

Thousands took part in the Aylesford pilgrimages and processions. The buildings had been extended, with guest-rooms, workshops, a spacious outdoor church. New statuary and artworks abounded. It may not have struck me at the time, but it has certainly struck me since, that a visitor knowing nothing of Christianity might have supposed this complex beside the Medway to a Goddess-temple. One of the first things seen on arrival was a great statue of the virgin in the outdoor church, and she stood alone, with no Christ-child anywhere near.

Discovering the Goddess

In that ambience I wrote much of my book on Glastonbury, *King Arthur's Avalon*, which, incidentally, Graves reviewed. A topic that had to be explored was the legend of the Holy Grail. There is probably no singly explanation of it, and, as I now know, scholars discussing the strange medieval literature tend to be selective and to ignore what does not support their theories. As a result even I, a rank amateur, noticed things which their interpretations had seldom brought out. One was an apparent pre-Christian background in female fertility symbolism. Another was an obscure but, I thought, significant link between the Grail and Mary, who is sometimes said to have been present in company with it. I learned also that the original church at Glastonbury, built – according to legend – by the Grail's custodian Joseph of Arimathea, was dedicated to her. There was an interweaving, though I was far from forming coherent ideas about it.

For some years, nothing further, apart from a few cautious Goddess allusions in my other books. Then I contributed some articles to the encyclopedia *man, Myth and Magic* (1970-2), including one on Virgin Births. Richard Cavendish, the editor, acted as literary adviser to the publishers Routledge and Kegan Paul. Would I be interested, he asked, in writing a history of the Church's cult of Mary? I had considered the idea myself. The few treatments known to me were written by Catholics with an eye to devotion or apologetics. It seemed to me that there was scope for a new study, more balanced, more exploratory. I submitted an outline and the book was contracted for.

I thought at first it could be a straightforward, consecutive account, from the dawn of Christianity to the present day. This turned out to be impossible. Mary's cult could not be understood as simply the promotion, legitimate or otherwise, of a Gospel character. Graves and Aylesford together had shown me that the Goddess presence was inescapable. Long preliminaries would be required before Mary could be brought on the stage at all.

Discovering the Goddess

Furthermore, while the Catholic authors might be right in spirit, the way they put their case was palpably wrong. They justified the worship of Jesus's mother ('worship', of course, not in the sense reserved for God) on the grounds that she was uniquely close to him. But I realized that whatever her status might be in heaven, the Gospels failed to show such a closeness on earth. If anything, after the birth-and-childhood stories they suggested estrangements, and a lack of interest in Mary in apostolic tradition.

And it went on like that. Early Christian texts, I found, had little in them that attested a special veneration for her, and nothing that portrayed her in Father Malachy's style as a celestial patroness able to hear and answer prayer. Mary-worship flowered in the Church quite swiftly and dramatically after three and a half centuries of silence, and, so far as the records go, it came from nowhere. This was a mystery which believers and unbelievers alike evaded. For me, it was crucial. I sensed an irruption of something far senior – female divinity. That topic could not be confined to the book's preliminaries, to the time before Christ. Mary's cult was a product within the church's framework of what might be described as a Goddess-shaped yearning among the faithful, which a purely God-centred religion had left unsatisfied. How did this come about?

When doing the actual writing, I found that the probing of the mystery was a long-drawn business. I used up most of my space getting to A.D. 431. In that year, amid wild public acclamation, a Church council at Ephesus acknowledged Mary as Mother of God, after which everything could follow with official approval. The publishers allowed me to go ahead, but the resulting book, *The Virgin* (1976, re-issued with a new preface 1988) was quite differently proportioned from the original plan.

An idea which I aired, picking up a hint from an Italian historian, was that devotion to the Virgin started in a separate milieu outside the Church, and forced its way in because of popular need. There is documentation for a sect of women who worshipped Mary as divine and as Queen of Heaven (a Goddess title thousands of years old) before Christians went even part of the way. Perhaps an influence came from that quarter. I may have ventured too far in my conjectures. Still, Andrew M. Greeley, the well-known American priest, sociologist and novelist, in a book of his own entitled *The Mary Myth*, was kind enough to comment:

> Geoffrey Ashe has the best available summary of the historical information available to use presently. His thesis about a popular Mariology that preceded the official cult (and about which the official Church has some doubts at first) is persuasive... It also seems reasonable to agree with Ashe - at least until later research proves him wrong - that the turning point was the triumph of popular devotion over official hesitation at the Council of Ephesus.

Another American, Michael P. Carroll, in an academic study *The Cult of the Virgin Mary*, describes *The Virgin* as 'the only work I know of that tries to account for the historical origins of the Mary cult using a reasonably systematic methodology'. He is unwilling to accept my notion about the sect of women, but, in a later chapter, he says the following:

> Let us reconsider the Ashe hypothesis that the relatively sudden of the Mary cult suggests that the cult derives from the sudden absorption into the Church of a group of Mary worshippers... He might well be right in believing that support for the cult was connected with absorption into the Church of some new group or groups. What makes this line of reasoning so appealing is that even conventional histories of the Church make it clear that the fourth century A.D. (the period just prior to the emergence of the Mary cult) was a period in which a variety of new groups were absorbed into the Church.

Discovering the Goddess

Carroll is more explicit than I was about a Goddess irruption. It was due, he thinks, to a flood of converts who included many worshippers of Cybele, the Great Mother. Obliged to give her up, they fastened on Mary as the sole Christian figure who could take over the role of a female deity. From there the cult expanded.

As to the exact process, I do not care much whether Carroll is right or I am right. Maybe we both are. The nature of the event is what matters. Catholic Christianity is a composite, re-shaped in the fifth century by the entry of a Goddess factor. That does not invalidate it. One of my clerical reviewers made the astounding charge that I was trying to 'explain Our Lady away'. As between Christian belief and unbelief, the argument in fact is impartial. A believer is quite at liberty to view Mary as a living being, exalted infinitely beyond her mortal limits, who assumed Goddess attributes in response to human needs and the Goddess-shaped yearning, when new pressures made them irresistible in the Church.

At the time of writing I was only marginally aware of such groups as the Fellowship of Isis, already taking root in Ireland, and of authors like Elizabeth Gould Davis who were promoting a revived Goddess interest from a feminist standpoint. Then a woman from Santa Cruz, California, happened to visit me and urged that University of California Extension ought to sponsor a seminar on *The Virgin*. Her name was Carolyn Shaefer. When she returned to Santa Cruz, and put forward her proposal, a realization rapidly dawned that several women historians and anthropologists were working along related lines. Terms such as 'Women's Spirituality' and 'Goddess-Consciousness' were coming into vogue. Merlin Stone, author of *When God was a Woman*, was making her voice heard, and so were Anne Kent Rush, Charlene Spretnak and others. The net was cast wider, and the result was a conference entitled 'The Great Goddess Re-Emerging'. About five hundred attended, the vast majority being women, some of them decidedly militant. I just survived as the solitary male speaker.

To get a visa, I had to go to the U.S. Embassy with a form giving details. I still remember my dialogue with the official.

> Official: What sort of a conference is this, Mr Ashe?
> Me: I suppose you could call it an anthropological conference.
> Him (having read further): 'The Great Goddess Re-Emerging'. What's that?
> Me: Well, some people think God is moving into the background a bit, and the Goddess is coming forward.
> Him: You don't mean to say we're getting Women's Lib in religion!
> Me: Yes – especially on the West Coast.
> Him: I suppose if it's going to happen anywhere it'll be on the West Coast. I hope you're going to tell them God is a man.

I didn't, and it would not have gone down well. The programme included rituals and meditations and dances, acts of worship in fact. The full-blown Goddess revival may be said to have begun there, at Santa Cruz, in 1978.

Despite a variety of activities since, the Goddess has been slow to penetrate higher education. I gave my first tentative course at Portland State twelve years after the Santa Cruz event. Repeated and elaborated each summer, it has remained, so far as I know, the only university Goddess course anywhere. The emphasis was and is, as I said, upon myth and history. However, a kind of sequel is taking shape treating recent and present day aspects, Goddess-worship as a living phenomenon, as it has become in the Pacific states and elsewhere – to the distress, apparently, of the Pope.

Discovering the Goddess

What can be said about it today? It retains a feminist outlook; as a rule, however, not a narrow or jaundiced one. Some Goddess-worshippers are still anti-male, and regard the great Lady as a deity for women only. These are in a minority. Ceremonies are held at which priestesses preside, but both sexes attend them. In my classes, while women students predominate, there have always been a few men, and they tend to be among the liveliest and best-informed.

One feature of the Goddess religion, a feature with social and political bearings, is its long perspective. It is not, exponents insist, a thing of today merely, or yesterday either. Up to a point this is obvious – Greek and Roman goddesses are familiar enough – but we are asked to look far beyond the point. Thus the Californian witch Starhawk, whose version of her Craft is a form of Goddess-worship, tells us it is the oldest religion on earth, with roots in the Palaeolithic age. Many others say much the same. Scholarly support has come from Marija Gimbutas, an archaeologist who is highly respected though not universally agreed with. Her huge illustrated books *The Language of the Goddess* and *The Civilization of the Goddess* have become virtually sacred texts.

According to those who follow her lead, there was once a Goddess era when deity was female rather than male. As a matter of fact, Graves went further thirty-odd years ago – or at any rate, took a more dogmatic tone – with the unqualified dictum 'Ancient Europe had no gods'. This is hard to substantiate from existing myths, European or otherwise; even 'in the beginning' there is nearly always a male entity around; and Goddess advocates admit there were gods as far back as proof can reach. But the gods, it is said, evolved out of the primordial Great Mother who contained both sexes within herself, and for a long time they were subordinate. As for the primordial Mother, evidence or reputed evidence is scattered through much of Europe and northern Asia. The best-known exhibits are female figurines sometimes dubbed Venuses, though Gimbutas objects. Several of them date back to 20,000 B.C. or further. Sceptics insist that these artifacts may be simply talismans, even dolls. Gimbutas, however, not only explains them as Goddess images but builds up a prehistoric network related to them, interpreting a medley of other imagery in suitable terms. Chevron patterns, wavy lines, spirals, and may birds and animals, are all made out to be linked with the Goddess and testimony to her worship. Well, perhaps. The case is ingenious and sometimes persuasive.

If the Palaeolithic age is ambiguous, the Neolithic and early Bronze ages are more encouraging: especially in the Middle East and south-eastern Europe, and especially after the beginnings of agriculture, in the seventh millennium B.C. Undeniable goddess-figures show themselves in art and myth. After about 3000 B.C., written matter puts names to some of them, such as Inanna, the Sumerian Queen of Heaven and Earth. Though perhaps already somewhat downgraded when she comes into view, she is still vastly more important than the later female occupants of Zeus's Olympus.

In the Goddess era, its advocates claim, life was different...and here a real battle is joined. It was a time of balance between the sexes. Society was not matriarchal in the sense of women ruling instead of men (here too Graves went further, saying it was; his successors are more moderate). But while not matriarchal it was sexually equal. Riane Eisler has coined the term 'gylanic', derived from the the first syllable of the Greek words for 'women' and 'man'. Early Minoan Crete, in the eyes of Goddess enthusiasts a near paradise, is held up as an achievement of gylanic society and a proof of its glory.

Crete, in its early phase, was powerful, and non-violence is said to have been characteristic of the Goddess era, on the grounds that violence is a product of male supremacy. That is called 'patriarchy' and, the story continues (in defiance of considerable scholarship), was imposed on Europe by migrant peoples from the steppes. They brought horses, they brought warfare, and they brought macho male gods, their homeland having been an exception in the Goddess's world. It was an eventual ethnic fusion under their dominance that hoisted gods like Zeus to the top. The Goddess was subordinated. She was split up into separate, increasingly functional goddesses far less than herself. Mythology was re-written in the interests of the new pantheon.

Patriarchy, meaning the rule of men and the subjection of women, went with this change and has been flourishing ever since. Christianity and Islam pushed the religious shift to the limit, affirming one Almighty Father who reigns alone, and both have kept women down, with little or no hindrance from such modifications as the cult of Mary. Central to the Goddess movement is the task of exposing this long-term trend.

The movement is involved, not only with ritual and spirituality, but with various causes. One is a fairly constructive feminism, pressing for sexual equality, and fostering new departures in art and poetry. Others take the form of campaigns against ecological evils blamed on male supremacy. The Goddess is interested in 'green' activities, and in the protection of wildlife; after all, one of her chief ancient guises was as Mistress of Animals. Goddess-worship is a religion of this life and this world. In England, some have linked it with a revamped mythos of Glastonbury, going behind familiar themes like the Grail legend to detect an original sacredness as a Goddess sanctuary...the interweaving I glimpsed long ago. Notable here is the work of a local dramatist, Kathy Jones.

How much of the ideology is valid? While teaching one of my courses at Portland State I was writing a book called *Dawn Behind the Dawn*, examining a problem in prehistory. I was struck by the fact that a miscellany of confused data did seem to make sense in the light of Goddess theories. With reservations, I can accept the case for a far-off era of female deity, though the reasons for its supplanting are probably more complex than the theorists think. There is no need to debate whether the Goddess was literally one, in a Palaeolithic or Neolithic or Bronze age monotheism, with an intercommunion of cults. Psychological oneness is enough, the *Ewig-Weibliche* manifested in different ways, with a vitality that prevented total oblivion when male gods became ascendant. History discloses a lurking pressure that could never be nullified, even when 'patriarchal' systems attempted it. The Goddess made a partial re-entry into Judaism as the female Wisdom of *Proverbs* 8:22-31 and several apocryphal passages, a mysterious being who says she was God's assistant in creation, though *Genesis* is silent about her. And an overwhelming popular thrust re-enthroned female deity in the Christian system, after three and a half centuries of resistance to it, in the shape of the exalted Virgin. It seems clear to me that something senior, once dominant, and inextinguishable, was indeed at work. Behind both Wisdom as personified, and Mary as exalted, specific goddess-figures are in fact discernible.

I am not so sure about the Goddess enthusiasts' package deal. I am not so sure about that sexually-balanced society, that 'gylany' over which, they maintain, the Goddess presided. Where is the evidence? True, the Goddess in her various forms had priestesses, so a substantial number of women enjoyed a status that was lost when the gods prevailed. Again, in some societies there were women who held power *ex officio*. A Celtic queen was equal to her consort or even superior; she could reign in her own right, she could lead armies, she could take lovers as the king could take concubines. But while the known facts about antiquity point to *some* women being privileged – and, if you will, because of Goddess-worship – they nowhere seem to show that *all* women were on a level with men. Artists in Crete portrayed aristocratic ladies who don't look at all repressed. But so did English portrait-painters in the eighteenth and nineteenth centuries. Their work does not imply that English society was other than patriarchal. It was very patriarchal indeed.

Marija Gimbutas, in *The Civilization of the Goddess*, says the gylanic society existed, and her disciples echo her and claim that the book gives proof. It doesn't. She offers almost no positive evidence, and in, in effect, contradicts herself. After ranging through masses of archaeological data, she comes to this conclusion:

> We visualize Old European society organized around a theacratic, communal temple community, and a higher female status in religious life. This was an endogamous society guided by a highly respected elder – Great Mother of the clan and her brother or uncle, with a council of women as a governing body. The structure was matrilineal, with succession to leadership and inheritance within the female line.

So what she arrives at on her own evidence is a scattering of local élites of privileged women. As far as it goes, it suggests matriarchy, not equality. But in truth, even on Gimbutas's showing, there is no real implication as to the relation between the sexes in general, or who was boss in the household or workplace. Society may have been gylanic, or it may have been vastly more various and complex. We simply don't know.

That harmonious Goddess past, with no inbuilt male mastery, savours a little too much of wishful thinking. It looks like yet another version of the perennial and persistent myth of a Golden Age – this time, a feminist version. To be sure, it would be pleasant to believe in it, if only proof that a gylanic society is possible, and might therefore be reconstituted. Indeed, a Goddess advocate might turn the criticism round, and argue that mythical Golden Ages embody faint memories of the real one, the age of the Goddess. Monica Sjöö actually does so, with an unconscious echo of Dante, who hints that the mythical Golden Ages are dim recollections of the Garden of Eden. However, this is all speculative. The Goddess's Golden Age may have existed. We cannot in honesty go further. Not yet, anyhow.

Within its group of adherents, the Neo-Goddess religion has reinstated something suppressed or perverted for millennia, and in the process it has brought back much that is wise, good, beautiful: as witness such works as *Sophia* by the Celticist Caitlín Matthews (spiritedly erudite, a little apart from the mainstream) and *The Once and Future Goddess* by the art historian Elinor Gadon. As to this there is no doubt, whatever questions overhang the bolder assertions. Still, how important is it? Should it be taken seriously as a major movement, hardly thus far, but in prospect?

I believe it should. To the extent that religion survives at all, Goddess-worship may be the key to a Next Step beyond present Christianity. That is a sweeping claim which must immediately be qualified. The Neo-Goddess religion may be the key, but it is not equipped, not as it stands, to be the Next Step itself.

The most obvious drawback is that its appeal is chiefly to women, and while men may learn to accept a female divinity (after all, women long since accepted a male one), the change will not be rapid. Another reason, less obvious, is the too frequent reliance on wishful speculation and flawed scholarship: the system is vulnerable, open to discrediting. Such weaknesses in it can be remedied and probably will be. A graver obstacle is the attitude of its shriller exponents to the Christianity which it might, in theory, supersede. They feud against the faith of the churches as patriarchal, they dismiss even the Mary cult as a priestly fraud, and, in the process, they go into contortions and acrobatics of hate that stultify their own case. Broadly speaking, when they refuse to face the god in Christianity – including its unforced hold on the loyalty and devotion of women – they are evading manifest fact, and when they denounce the evil, they are either attacking crimes and corruptions that have long been notorious and are no revelation, or inventing other crimes and corruptions that they have to destroy, and they never will.

If there is to be a Next Step, it cannot come through destruction. The new thing must absorb Christianity and revalue it, as Christianity absorbed and revalued so much that went before, drawing on the Judaism it claimed to fulfil, on Greek philosophy, on pagan myths and cults which it damned yet assimilated. Today, the Goddess's re-emergence may be what is required to make a Next Step possible. But the new thing would surely have to be a religion of God *and* Goddess, in whatever sense those terms may be understood (more radical, certainly, than some Christians' belated discovery that god has a 'feminine aspect' or is our 'Father-Mother'). Granted a theology of partnership, doors would open.

Many practitioners of present day witchcraft – 'Wicca' – say they are there already, working with a Female-and-Male, Goddess-and-God polarity, if with more emphasis on the Goddess. However, they have little interest in proselytizing. That eminent witch Starhawk draws a distinction. The doctrine she teaches can act as an inspiration and catalyst without any attempt at universality.

> To return to the circle [of inner and outer harmony] does not necessarily mean to embrace Witchcraft specifically. I hope the religion of the future will be multifaceted, growing out of many traditions. Perhaps we will see a new cult of the Virgin Mary and a revival of the ancient Hebrew Goddess. Native American traditions and Afro-American traditions may flourish in an atmosphere in which they are given the respect they deserve. Eastern religions will inevitably change as they grow in the West – and part of that change may be in the roles they assign to women.

Discovering the Goddess

Those who deride Wicca's pretensions to antiquity may see nothing here but Starhawk making it up as she goes along. I would not agree. But we can look in better known, better documented quarters. The British Isles have the pagan Celtic tradition. It does not offer a central, focusing theology on gender-partnership lines, but it does offer rich potentialities for it. To go further afield, India actually provides such a theology, the Tantric, which is a God-and-Goddess system many centuries old.

A great mystic and reformer whom it influenced, Ramakrishna (1836-86), was an ardent Goddess revivalist long before anyone in the West. He brings us back to the starting-point. The Chicago Parliament of Religions in 1993 commemorated the previous one in 1893. Among the speakers then was Ramakrishna's ablest disciple, Vivekananda. His lectures during his American visit made a deep impression on William James when James's thoughts were moving towards his pioneer study *The Varieties of Religious Experience*. Vivekananda, expanding the message of his own Goddess-intoxicated guru, conceived the religion of the future as 'the sum of it all, with more beyond'. Perhaps that was an early foreshadowing of the Next Step, towards which the present Goddess revival, by recovering so much that was lost, is mapping a path.

Select Bibliography

Marc Alexander: *British Folklore, Myths and Legends*, Weidenfeld & Nicolson 1982
Karen Armstrong: *The Gospel According to Woman: Christianity's Creation of the Sex War in the West*, Pan 1987
Geoffrey Ashe: *Mythology of the British Isles*, Methuen 1990
—. *The Virgin: Mary's Cult and the Re-emergence of the Goddess*, Arkana 1987
—. ed: *The Quest For Arthur's Britain*, Pall Mall Press 1968
Ean Begg: *The Cult of the Black Virgin*, Routledge 1985
Pamela Berger: *The Goddess Obscured*, Robert Hale 1988
Bruce Bernard: *The Queen of Heaven*, Macdonald Orbis 1987
Janet & Colin Bord: *Ancient Mysteries of Britain*, Paladin 1987
—. *Mysterious Britain*, Paladin 1974
Robert Briffault: *The Mothers: A Study of the origins of Sentiments and Institutions*, Allen & Unwin, 3 vols, 1927
Ron Cameron: *The Other Gospels*, Lutterworth Press, Surrey 1983
Joseph Campbell: *The Power of Myth*, with Bill Moyers, ed. Betty Sue Flowers, Doubleday, New York 1988
Michael P. Carroll: *The Cult of the Virgin Mary*, Princeton University Press, New Jersey 1986
J.E. Cirlot: *A Dictionary of Symbols,* Routledge 1981
Mary Daly: *Beyond God the Father*, Women's Press 1985
Michael Dames: *The Avebury Cycle,* Thames & Hudson 1976
Lene Dressen-Coenders, ed: *Saints and She-Devils*, Rubicon Press 1987
Mircea Eliade: *A History of Religious Ideas*, I, Collins 1979
—. *Patterns in Comparative Religion*, Sheed & Ward 1958
—. *Myths, Dreams and Mysteries*, Harper & Row, New York 1975
J.G..Frazer: *The Golden Bough*, abridged edition, Macmillan 1922/59
Elinor Gadon: *The Once and Future Goddess*, Aquarian Press 1990
Marija Gimbutas: *The Language of the Goddess*, Thomas & Hudson 1989

Discovering the Goddess

Robert Graves: *The White Goddess*, Faber 1961
—. *Mammon and the Black Goddess*, Cassell 1965
—. *Collected Poems 1975*, Cassell 1975
—. *Between Moon and Moon: Selected Letters of Robert Graves 1946-72*, ed. Paul O'Prey, Hutchinson 1984
—. *Conversations with Robert Graves*, ed. Frank Kersnowski, University of Mississippi Press, Jackson 1989
M. Esther Harding: *Women's Mysteries, Rider 1989*
Edward Hulme: *Symbolism in Christian Art*, Blandford Press, Poole 1976
Jacob de Voraigne: *The Golden Legend*, ed. Ellis, 7 vols, J.M. Dent 1900
William James: *The Varieties of Religious Experience*, Collins 1958
Patrick J. Keane: *A Wild Civility: Interactions in the Poetry of Robert Graves*, University Press of Missouri, Columbia 1980
Karl Kerenyi: *Goddess of the Sun and Moon*, Spring publications, Dallas 1989
David Kinsley: *The Goddess's Mirror: Visions of the Divine From East and West*, State University of New York Press 1989
James Marchant: *The Madonna: An Anthology*, Burns, Oates & Washbourne, n.d.
Caitlin Matthews, ed: *Elements of the Goddess*, Element Books, Dorset 1989
John Matthews, ed. *An Arthurian Reader*, Aquarian Press, Northants 1991
Patrick Murray: *Mary: A Marian Anthology*, Verites, Dublin 1979
Erich Neumann: *The Great Mother*, Princeton University Press, New Jersey 1972
Shirley Nicholson, ed. *The Goddess Re-awakening: The Goddess Principle Today*, Theosophical Publishing House, New York 1989
Christopher O'Donnell: *Life in the Spirit and Mary*, Wilmington 1981
Ginette Paris: *Pagan Meditations*, Spring Publications, Dallas 1988
Philip Rawson: *The Art of Tantra*, Thames & Hudson 1973
Peter Redgrove: *The Black Goddess and the Sixth Sense*, Bloomsbury 1987
Penelope Shuttle & Peter Redgrove: *The Wise Wound*, Paladin/ Grafton 1978/86
Monica Sjöo & Barbara Mor: *The Great Cosmic Mother*, Harper & Row, San Francisco 1987
Ninian Smart: *The World's Religions*, Cambridge University Press 1989
C. Spretnak, ed: *The Politics of Women's Spirituality: Essays on the Rise of Spiritual Power Within the Feminist Movement*, Anchor Press, Garden City, New York 1982
Starhawk: *The Spiral Dance*, Harper & Row, San Francisco 1979
—. *Dreaming the Dark*, Beacon Press, Boston 1982
R.J. Stewart: *The Mystic Life of Merlin*, Routledge 1986
—. ed. *The Book of Merlin*, Blandford Press, Poole 1987
Marina Warner: *Alone Of All Her Sex: The Myth and Cult of the Virgin Mary*, Picador 1985
—. *Monuments and Maidens*, Weidenfeld & Nicholson 1985

Discovering the Goddess

Edward C. Whitmont: *Return of the Goddess*, Routledge 1987
Marion Woodman: *The Pregnant Virgin: A Process of Psychological Transformation*, Inner City Books, Toronto, Canada 1985

Illustrations

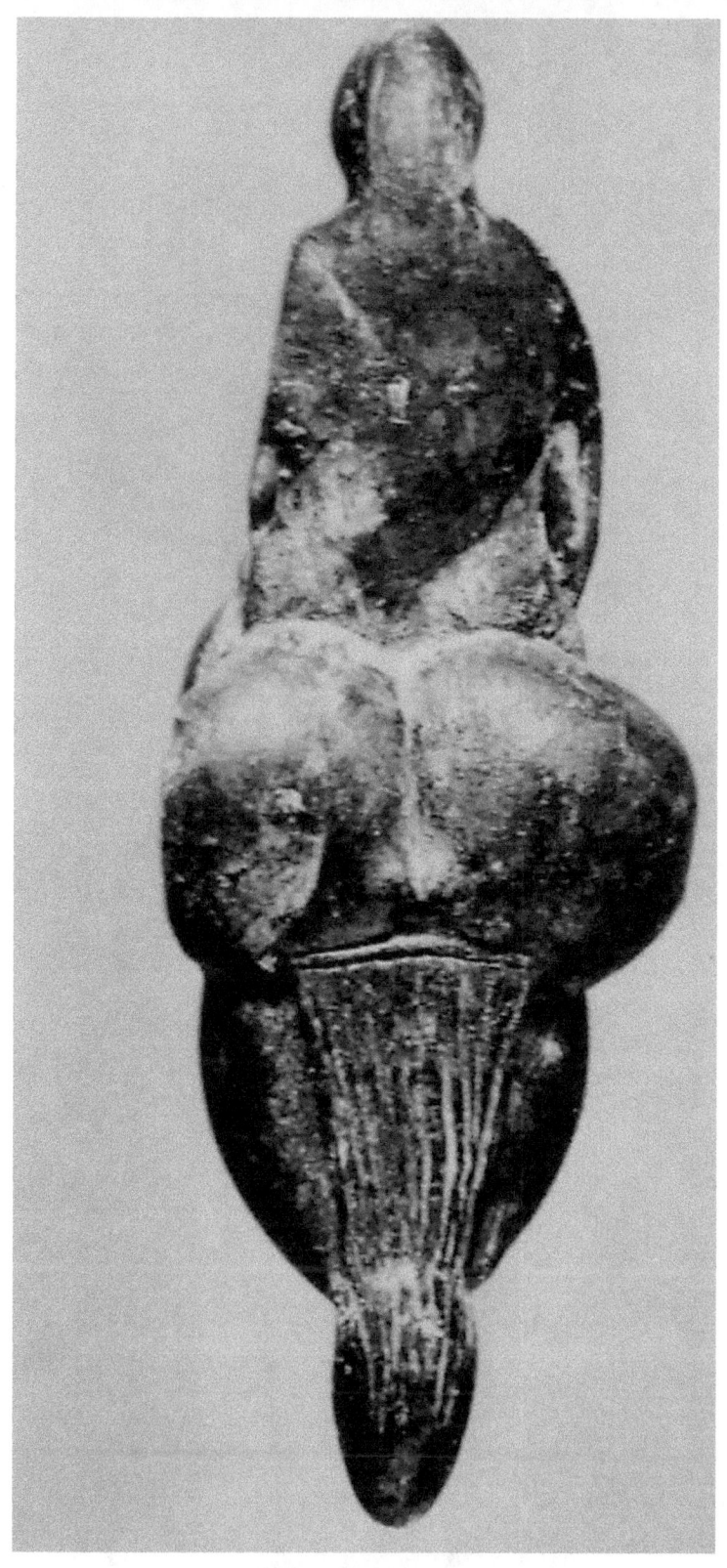

Venus of Willendorf, prehistoric, Vienna

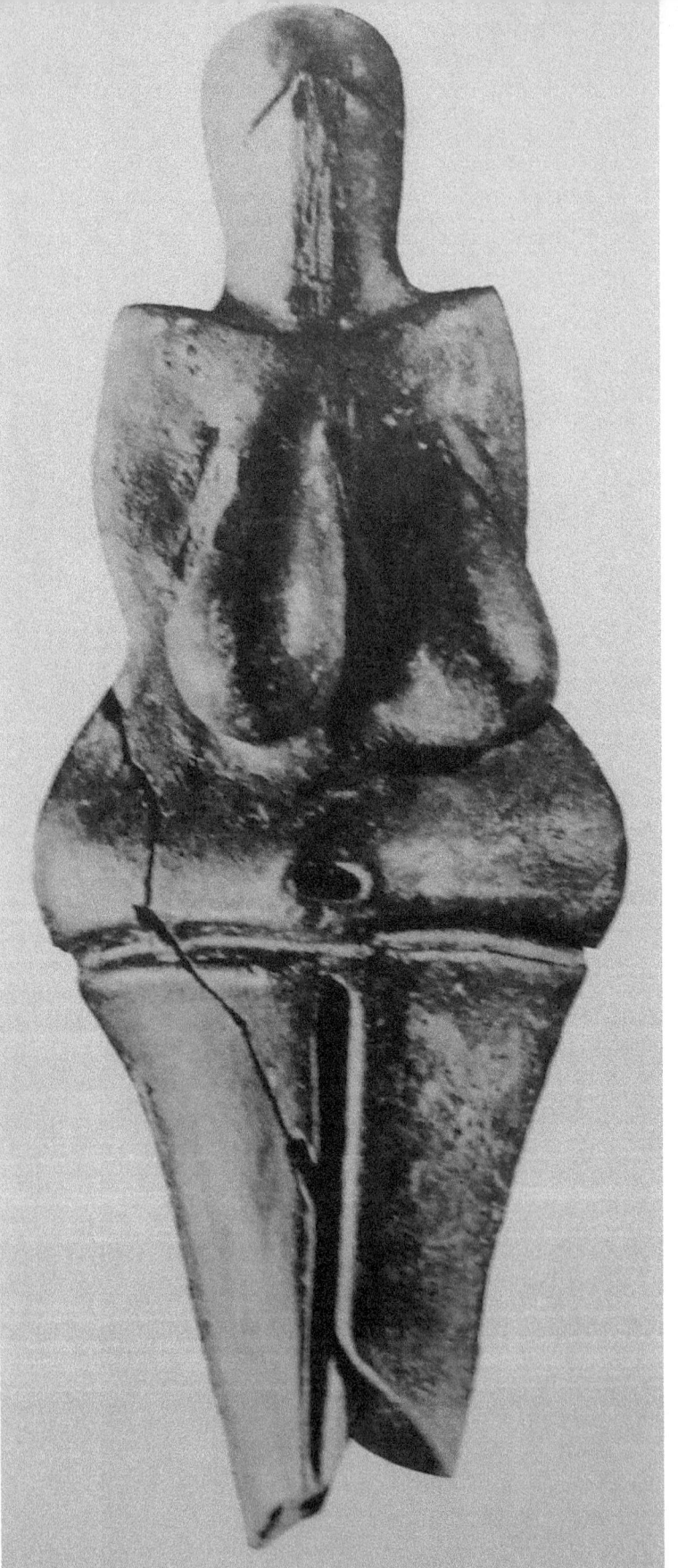

Stone Venus, prehistoric.

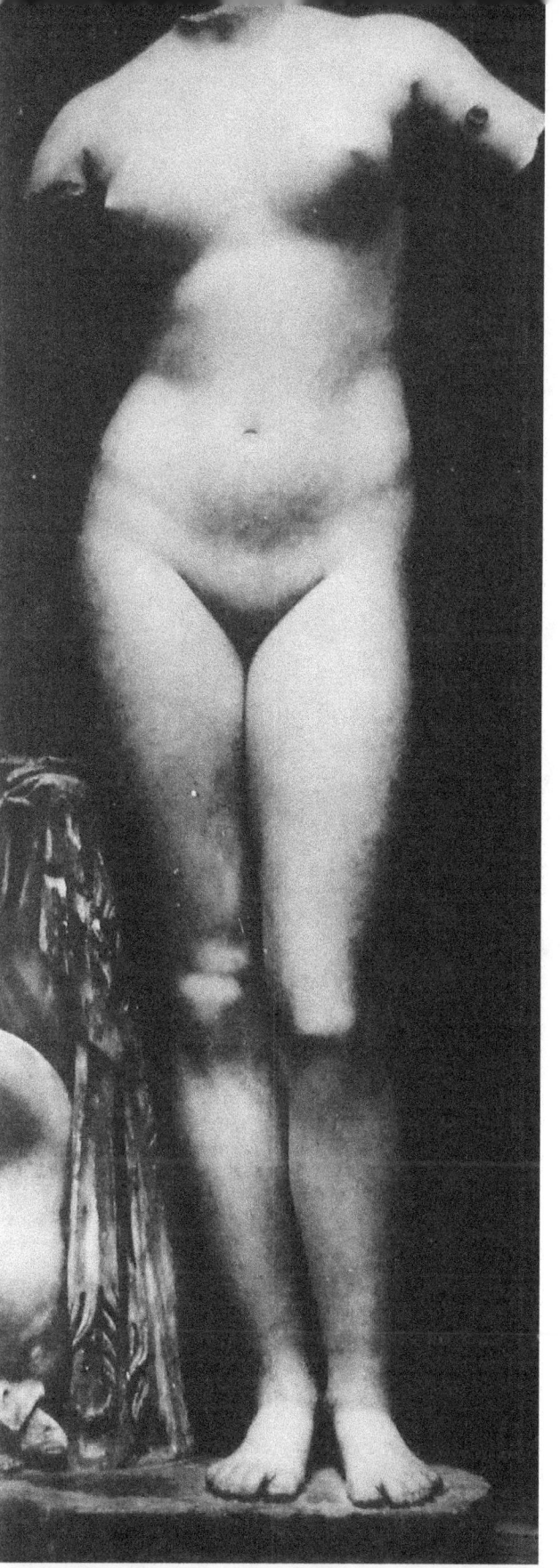

Aphrodite of Cyrene

Fra Angelico, The Annunciation, San Marco, Florence

Fra Filippo Lippi, The Adoration of the Virgin, Berlin, detail

Andreas Mantegna, Madonna and Child Enthroned, 1457-60, Verona

Piero, Madonna della Misericordia, Sanepulchro

Sandro Botticelli, *Pietà*, Museo Poldi Pezzoli, Milan

Anna Mendieta's Goddess art of the
19770s

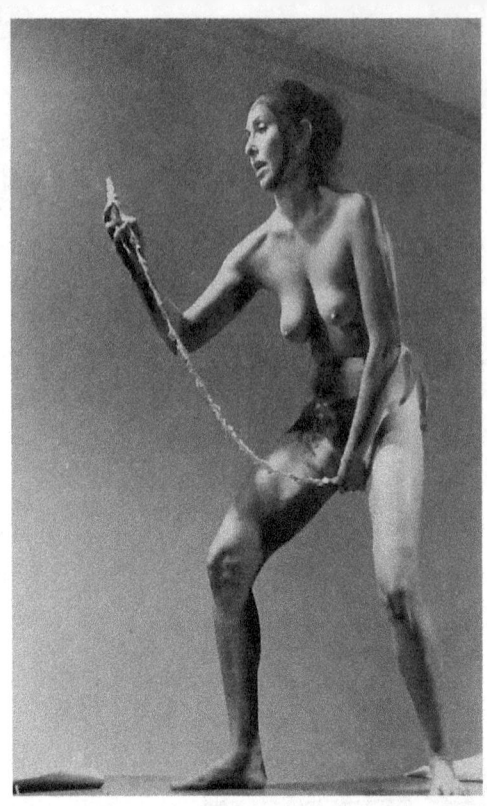

Examples of Goddess-related feminist performance art of the 1970s.

Carolee Schneemann, Interior Scroll, 1975, left.

Mary Beth Edelson, Grapceva Cave, 1977, below.

J.R.R. Tolkien
The Books, The Films, The Whole Cultural Phenomenon

by Jeremy Mark Robinson

A new critical study of J.R.R. Tolkien, creator of Middle-earth and author of *The Lord of the Rings, The Hobbit* and *The Silmarillion*, among other books.

This new critical study explores Tolkien's major writings (*The Lord of the Rings, The Hobbit, Beowulf: The Monster and the Critics, The Letters, The Silmarillion* and *The History of Middle-earth* volumes); Tolkien and fairy tales; the mythological, political and religious aspects of Tolkien's Middle-earth; the critics' response to Tolkien's fiction over the decades; the Tolkien industry (merchandizing, toys, role-playing games, posters, Tolkien societies, conferences and the like); Tolkien in visual and fantasy art; the cultural aspects of The Lord of the Rings (from the 1950s to the present); Tolkien's fiction's relationship with other fantasy fiction, such as C.S. Lewis and *Harry Potter*; and the TV, radio and film versions of Tolkien's books, including the 2001-03 Hollywood interpretations of *The Lord of the Rings*.

This new book draws on contemporary cultural theory and analysis and offers a sympathetic and illuminating (and sceptical) account of the Tolkien phenomenon. This book is designed to appeal to the general reader (and viewer) of Tolkien: it is written in a clear, jargon-free and easily-accessible style.

754pp   ISBN 1-86171-057-7   £25.00 / $37.50

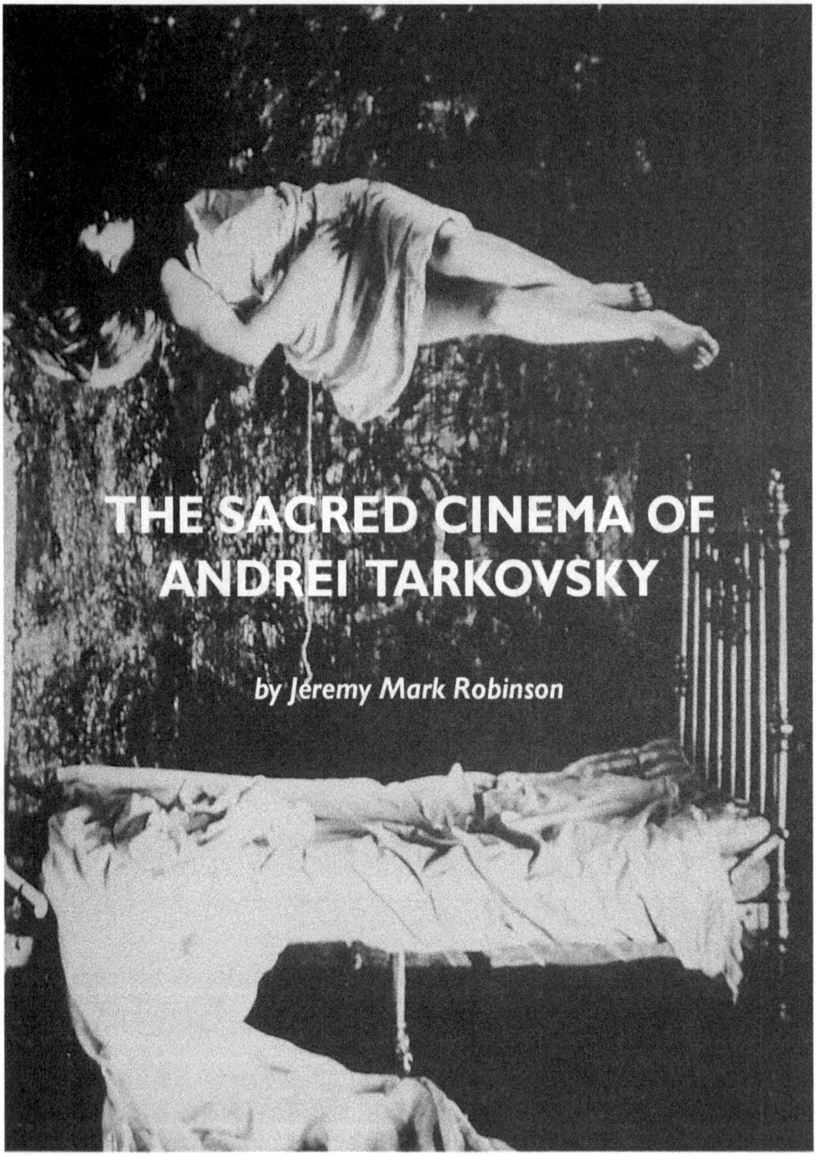

THE SACRED CINEMA OF ANDREI TARKOVSKY

by Jeremy Mark Robinson

A new study of the Russian filmmaker Andrei Tarkovsky (1932-1986), director of seven feature films, including *Andrei Roublyov, Mirror, Solaris, Stalker* and *The Sacrifice*.

This is one of the most comprehensive and detailed studies of Tarkovsky's cinema available. Every film is explored in depth, with scene-by-scene analyses. All aspects of Tarkovsky's output are critiqued, including editing, camera, staging, script, budget, collaborations, production, sound, music, performance and spirituality. Tarkovsky is placed with a European New Wave tradition of filmmaking, alongside directors like Ingmar Bergman, Carl Theodor Dreyer, Pier Paolo Pasolini and Robert Bresson.

An essential addition to film studies.

Illustrations: 150 b/w, 4 colour. 682 pages. First edition. Hardback.

Publisher: Crescent Moon Publishing. Distributor: Gardners Books.

ISBN 1-86171-096-8 (9781861710963) £60.00 / $105.00

The Best of Peter Redgrove's Poetry
The Book of Wonders

by Peter Redgrove, edited and introduced by Jeremy Robinson

Poems of wet shirts and 'wonder-awakening dresses'; honey, wasps and bees; orchards and apples; rivers, seas and tides; storms, rain, weather and clouds; waterworks; labyrinths; amazing perfumes; the Cornish landscape (Penzance, Perranporth, Falmouth, Boscastle, the Lizard and Scilly Isles); the sixth sense and 'extra-sensuous perception'; witchcraft; alchemical vessels and laboratories; yoga; menstruation; mines, minerals and stones; sand dunes; mud-baths; mythology; dreaming; vulvas; and lots of sex magic. This book gathers together poetry (and prose) from every stage of Redgrove's career, and every book. It includes pieces that have only appeared in small presses and magazines, and in uncollected form.

'Peter Redgrove is really an extraordinary poet' (George Szirtes, *Quarto* magazine)
'Peter Redgrove is one of the few significant poets now writing... His 'means' are indeed brilliant and delightful. Technically he is a poet essentially of brilliant and unexpected images...he never disappoints' (Kathleen Raine, *Temenos* magazine).

240pp   ISBN 1-86171-063-1   2nd edition   £19.99 / $29.50

Sex–Magic–Poetry–Cornwall
A Flood of Poems

by Peter Redgrove. Edited with an essay by Jeremy Robinson

A marvellous collection of poems by one of Britain's best but underrated poets, Peter Redgrove. This book brings together some of Redgrove's wildest and most passionate works, creating a 'flood' of poetry. Philip Hobsbaum called Redgrove 'the great poet of our time', while Angela Carter said: 'Redgrove's language can light up a page.' Redgrove ranks alongside Ted Hughes and Sylvia Plath. He is in every way a 'major poet'. Robinson's essay analyzes all of Redgrove's poetic work, including his use of sex magic, natural science, menstruation, psychology, myth, alchemy and feminism.
A new edition, including a new introduction, new preface and new bibliography.

'Robinson's enthusiasm is winning, and his perceptive readings are supported by a very useful bibliography' (*Acumen* magazine)
'*Sex-Magic-Poetry-Cornwall* is a very rich essay... It is like a brightly-lighted box. (Peter Redgrove)
'This is an excellent selection of poetry and an extensive essay on the themes and theories of this unusual poet by Jeremy Robinson' (*Chapman* magazine)

220pp   New, 3rd edition   ISBN 1-86171-070-4   £14.99 / $23.50

THE ART OF ANDY GOLDSWORTHY

COMPLETE WORKS: SPECIAL EDITION
(PAPERBACK and HARDBACK)

by William Malpas

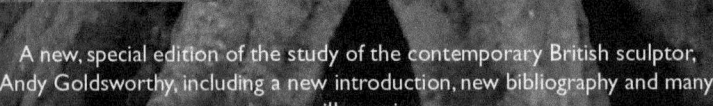

A new, special edition of the study of the contemporary British sculptor, Andy Goldsworthy, including a new introduction, new bibliography and many new illustrations.

This is the most comprehensive, up-to-date, well-researched and in-depth account of Goldsworthy's art available anywhere.

Andy Goldsworthy makes land art. His sculpture is a sensitive, intuitive response to nature, light, time, growth, the seasons and the earth. Goldsworthy's environmental art is becoming ever more popular: 1993's art book *Stone* was a bestseller; the press raved about Goldsworthy taking over a number of London West End art galleries in 1994; during 1995 Goldsworthy designed a set of Royal Mail stamps and had a show at the British Museum. Malpas surveys all of Goldsworthy's art, and analyzes his relation with other land artists such as Robert Smithson, Walter de Maria, Richard Long and David Nash, and his place in the contemporary British art scene.

The Art of Andy Goldsworthy discusses all of Goldsworthy's important and recent exhibitions and books, including the *Sheepfolds* project; the TV documentaries; *Wood* (1996); the New York Holocaust memorial (2003); and Goldsworthy's collaboration on a dance performance.

Illustrations: 70 b/w, 1 colour. 330 pages. New, special, 2nd edition.
Publisher: Crescent Moon Publishing. Distributor: Gardners Books.

ISBN 1-86171-059-3 (9781861710598) (Paperback) £25.00 / $44.00

ISBN 1-86171-080-1 (9781861710802) (Hardback) £60.00 / $105.00

CRESCENT MOON PUBLISHING

ARTS, PAINTING, SCULPTURE

The Art of Andy Goldsworthy: Complete Works(Pbk)
The Art of Andy Goldsworthy: Complete Works (Hbk)
Andy Goldsworthy in Close-Up (Pbk)
Andy Goldsworthy in Close-Up (Hbk)
Land Art: A Complete Guide
Richard Long: The Art of Walking
The Art of Richard Long: Complete Works (Pbk)
The Art of Richard Long: Complete Works (Hbk)
Richard Long in Close-Up
Land Art In the UK
Land Art in Close-Up
Installation Art in Close-Up
Minimal Art and Artists In the 1960s and After
Colourfield Painting
Land Art DVD, TV documentary
Andy Goldsworthy DVD, TV documentary
The Erotic Object: Sexuality in Sculpture From Prehistory to the Present Day
Sex in Art: Pornography and Pleasure in Painting and Sculpture
Postwar Art
Sacred Gardens: The Garden in Myth, Religion and Art
Glorification: Religious Abstraction in Renaissance and 20th Century Art
Early Netherlandish Painting
Leonardo da Vinci
Piero della Francesca
Giovanni Bellini
Fra Angelico: Art and Religion in the Renaissance
Mark Rothko: The Art of Transcendence
Frank Stella: American Abstract Artist
Jasper Johns: Painting By Numbers
Brice Marden
Alison Wilding: The Embrace of Sculpture
Vincent van Gogh: Visionary Landscapes
Eric Gill: Nuptials of God
Constantin Brancusi: Sculpting the Essence of Things
Max Beckmann
Egon Schiele: Sex and Death In Purple Stockings
Delizioso Fotografico Fervore: Works In Process 1
Sacro Cuore: Works In Process 2
The Light Eternal: J.M.W. Turner
The Madonna Glorified: Karen Arthurs

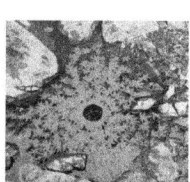

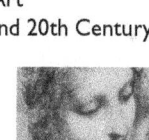

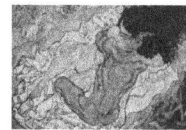

LITERATURE

J.R.R. Tolkien: The Books, The Films, The Whole Cultural Phenomenon
Harry Potter
Sexing Hardy: Thomas Hardy and Feminism
Thomas Hardy's *Tess of the d'Urbervilles*
Thomas Hardy's *Jude the Obscure*
Thomas Hardy: The Tragic Novels
Love and Tragedy: Thomas Hardy
The Poetry of Landscape in Hardy
Wessex Revisited: Thomas Hardy and John Cowper Powys
Wolfgang Iser: Essays
Petrarch, Dante and the Troubadours
Maurice Sendak and the Art of Children's Book Illustration
Andrea Dworkin
Cixous, Irigaray, Kristeva: The *Jouissance* of French Feminism
Julia Kristeva: Art, Love, Melancholy, Philosophy, Semiotics and Psychoanalysis
Hélène Cixous I Love You: The *Jouissance* of Writing
Luce Irigaray: Lips, Kissing, and the Politics of Sexual Difference
Peter Redgrove: Here Comes the Flood
Peter Redgrove: Sex-Magic-Poetry-Cornwall
Lawrence Durrell: Between Love and Death, East and West
Love, Culture & Poetry: Lawrence Durrell
Cavafy: Anatomy of a Soul
German Romantic Poetry: Goethe, Novalis, Heine, Hölderlin, Schlegel, Schiller
Feminism and Shakespeare
Shakespeare: Selected Sonnets
Shakespeare: Love, Poetry & Magic
The Passion of D.H. Lawrence
D.H. Lawrence: Symbolic Landscapes
D.H. Lawrence: Infinite Sensual Violence
Rimbaud: Arthur Rimbaud and the Magic of Poetry
The Ecstasies of John Cowper Powys
Sensualism and Mythology: The Wessex Novels of John Cowper Powys
Amorous Life: John Cowper Powys and the Manifestation of Affectivity (H.W. Fawkner)
Postmodern Powys: New Essays on John Cowper Powys (Joe Boulter)
Rethinking Powys: Critical Essays on John Cowper Powys
Paul Bowles & Bernardo Bertolucci
Rainer Maria Rilke
In the Dim Void: Samuel Beckett
Samuel Beckett Goes into the Silence
André Gide: Fiction and Fervour
Jackie Collins and the Blockbuster Novel
Blinded By Her Light: The Love-Poetry of Robert Graves
The Passion of Colours: Travels In Mediterranean Lands
Poetic Forms
The Dolphin-Boy

POETRY

The Best of Peter Redgrove's Poetry
Peter Redgrove: Here Comes The Flood
Peter Redgrove: Sex-Magic-Poetry-Cornwall
Ursula Le Guin: Walking In Cornwall
Dante: Selections From the Vita Nuova
Petrarch, Dante and the Troubadours
William Shakespeare: Selected Sonnets
Blinded By Her Light: The Love-Poetry of Robert Graves
Emily Dickinson: Selected Poems
Emily Brontë: Poems
Thomas Hardy: Selected Poems
Percy Bysshe Shelley: Poems
John Keats: Selected Poems
D.H. Lawrence: Selected Poems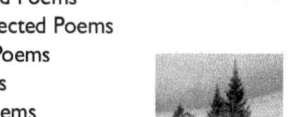
Edmund Spenser: Poems
John Donne: Poems
Henry Vaughan: Poems
Sir Thomas Wyatt: Poems
Robert Herrick: Selected Poems
Rilke: Space, Essence and Angels in the Poetry of Rainer Maria Rilke
Rainer Maria Rilke: Selected Poems
Friedrich Hölderlin: Selected Poems
Arseny Tarkovsky: Selected Poems
Arthur Rimbaud: Selected Poems
Arthur Rimbaud: A Season in Hell
Arthur Rimbaud and the Magic of Poetry
D.J. Enright: By-Blows
Jeremy Reed: Brigitte's Blue Heart
Jeremy Reed: Claudia Schiffer's Red Shoes
Gorgeous Little Orpheus
Radiance: New Poems
Crescent Moon Book of Nature Poetry
Crescent Moon Book of Love Poetry
Crescent Moon Book of Mystical Poetry
Crescent Moon Book of Elizabethan Love Poetry
Crescent Moon Book of Metaphysical Poetry
Crescent Moon Book of Romantic Poetry
Pagan America: New American Poetry

MEDIA, CINEMA, FEMINISM and CULTURAL STUDIES

J.R.R. Tolkien: The Books, The Films, The Whole Cultural Phenomenon
Harry Potter
Cixous, Irigaray, Kristeva: The *Jouissance* of French Feminism
Julia Kristeva: Art, Love, Melancholy, Philosophy, Semiotics and Psychoanalysis
Luce Irigaray: Lips, Kissing, and the Politics of Sexual Difference
Hélène Cixous I Love You: The *Jouissance* of Writing
Andrea Dworkin
'Cosmo Woman': The World of Women's Magazines
Women in Pop Music
Discovering the Goddess (Geoffrey Ashe)
The Poetry of Cinema
The Sacred Cinema of Andrei Tarkovsky (Pbk and Hbk)
Paul Bowles & Bernardo Bertolucci
Media Hell: Radio, TV and the Press
An Open Letter to the BBC
Detonation Britain: Nuclear War in the UK
Feminism and Shakespeare
Wild Zones: Pornography, Art and Feminism
Sex in Art: Pornography and Pleasure in Painting and Sculpture
Sexing Hardy: Thomas Hardy and Feminism

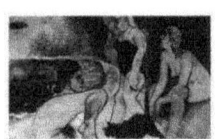

In my view *The Light Eternal* is among the very best of all the material I read on Turner. (Douglas Graham, director of the Turner Museum, Denver, Colorado)

The Light Eternal is a model monograph, an exemplary job. The subject matter of the book is beautifully organised and dead on beam. (Lawrence Durrell)

It is amazing for me to see my work treated with such passion and respect. (Andrea Dworkin)

Sex-Magic-Poetry-Cornwall is a very rich essay... It is like a brightly-lighted box. (Peter Redgrove)

CRESCENT MOON PUBLISHING
P.O. Box 393, Maidstone, Kent, ME14 5XU, United Kingdom.
01622-729593 (UK) 01144-1622-729593 (US) 0044-1622-729593 (other territories)
cresmopub@yahoo.co.uk   www.crescentmoon.org.uk

www.ingramcontent.com/pod-product-compliance
Lightning Source LLC
Chambersburg PA
CBHW061255040426
42444CB00010B/2392